Uncle Sam

by Anastasia Suen
illustrated by Matthew Skeens

PICTURE WINDOW BOOKS
Minneapolis, Minnesota

Special thanks to our advisers for their expertise:

Kevin Byrne, Ph.D., Professor of History
Gustavus Adolphus College, St. Peter, Minnesota

Terry Flaherty, Ph.D., Professor of English
Minnesota State University, Mankato

Editor: Jill Kalz
Designer: Abbey Fitzgerald
Page Production: Melissa Kes
Art Director: Nathan Gassman
Associate Managing Editor: Christianne Jones
The illustrations in this book were created digitally.
Photo Credit: Library of Congress, 23

Picture Window Books
151 Good Counsel Drive, P.O. Box 669
Mankato, MN 56002-0669
877-845-8392
www.picturewindowbooks.com

Library of Congress Cataloging-in-Publication Data
Suen, Anastasia.
Uncle Sam / by Anastasia Suen ; illustrated by Matthew Skeens.
p. cm. — (American symbols)
Includes index.
ISBN 978-1-4048-4706-4 (library binding)
1. Uncle Sam (Symbolic character)—Juvenile literature. 2. Wilson,
Samuel, 1766-1854—Juvenile literature. 3. United States—Biography—
Juvenile literature. I. Skeens, Matthew, ill. II. Title.
E179.S93 2008
398.20973'02—dc22   2008006342

Table of Contents

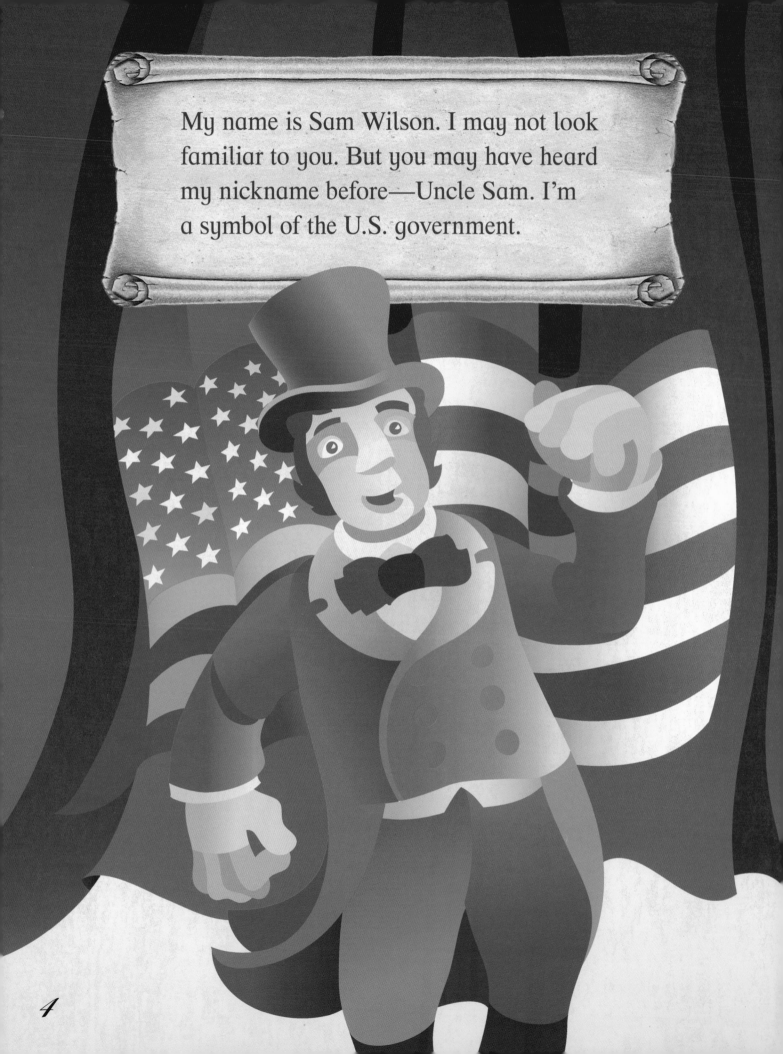

My name is Sam Wilson. I may not look familiar to you. But you may have heard my nickname before—Uncle Sam. I'm a symbol of the U.S. government.

How did I become Uncle Sam? It happened because of cartoons, a circus clown, and millions of posters.

Here's my story.

A Pair of Initials

During the War of 1812, my brother and I were meatpackers.
We packed meat in wooden barrels. The U.S. government then
sent the barrels to the soldiers. Each barrel was marked with the
letters *U.S.*, which stood for "United States."

Some soldiers thought *U.S.* stood for me, Sam Wilson, or "Uncle Sam." Soon the name Uncle Sam became a nickname for the government of the United States.

The United States and Uncle Sam have the same initials, *U.S.*

A Cartoon Character

In the early days of the United States, many magazines and newspapers had cartoons. The drawings focused on world events. Cartoonists wanted a character to stand for the United States.

English cartoonists used a character named John Bull to stand for their country. He wore a vest with an English flag on it.

Stars and Stripes

For years, U.S. cartoonists drew characters wearing stars and stripes. They drew Yankee Doodle. They drew Brother Jonathan, a character who was said to be named after Governor Jonathan Trumbull of Connecticut. Both of these characters were created during the Revolutionary War (1775–1783).

Brother
Jonathan

11

Uncle Sam

As the country grew, cartoonists created another character to symbolize the United States. They named him Uncle Sam. At first, Uncle Sam looked like Brother Jonathan. The two characters wore the same clothes: a top hat, a long coat with tails, and striped pants.

A Famous Clown

In the mid-1800s, some cartoonists started modeling Uncle Sam after a famous clown. The clown's name was Dan Rice. He wore red, white, and blue costumes.

By the 1860s, Dan Rice was so popular that he made more money per year than President Abraham Lincoln.

After the Civil War (1861–1865), a cartoonist named Thomas Nast gave Uncle Sam a new look. He made Uncle Sam look a little like President Abraham Lincoln. He drew a tall, thin man with a beard. Other cartoonists did the same.

Birthday Presents

In 1876, the United States turned 100 years old. To celebrate the country's birthday, people made and sold gifts of all kinds. Many items had pictures of Uncle Sam on them.

Songs were also written about Uncle Sam, including "Uncle Sam's Farm."

I Want You

One more artist had a say in how Uncle Sam looked. In 1916, James Montgomery Flagg drew himself as Uncle Sam. His drawing was on the cover of a magazine. Then it was printed on a U.S. Army poster. The poster urged people to join the Army during World War I (1914–1918).

The United States entered World War I in 1917, and the need for soldiers was great. More than 4 million copies of the "I Want You" poster were made between 1917 and 1918.

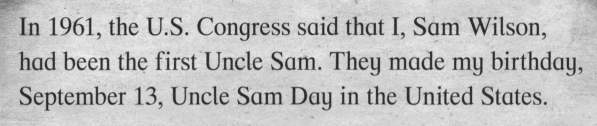

In 1961, the U.S. Congress said that I, Sam Wilson, had been the first Uncle Sam. They made my birthday, September 13, Uncle Sam Day in the United States.

That's the story of one of our country's most recognized symbols. I hope you enjoyed it!

Uncle Sam Facts

- Sam Wilson, the original Uncle Sam, was born in Arlington, Massachusetts, in 1766. He spent most of his life in Troy, New York, where he died in 1854.

- Before Uncle Sam, Brother Jonathan was a symbol of the United States. Brother Jonathan stood for a strong U.S. government but even stronger separate but equal states. Uncle Sam, on the other hand, stood for strong states but an even stronger U.S. government.

- James Montgomery Flagg was a gifted artist long before he drew Uncle Sam. He sold his first illustration at the age of 12. By age 15, he was working for two top magazine publishers.

Uncle Sam poster

Glossary

cartoonist — a person who draws cartoons

Civil War — (1861–1865) the battle between states in the North and South that led to the end of slavery in the United States

Congress — the group of people in the U.S. government who make laws

Revolutionary War — (1775–1783) the American Colonies' fight for freedom from Great Britain; the Colonies later became the United States of America

symbol — an object that stands for something else

War of 1812 — (1812–1815) the war between the United States and Great Britain over unfair British control of shipping; often called the "Second War of Independence"

World War I — (1914–1918) the war between the Central Powers (Germany, Austria-Hungary, and Turkey) and the Allied Powers (mainly France, Great Britain, Russia, Italy, Japan, and the United States)

To Learn More

More Books to Read

Banks, Kate. *Howie Bowles and Uncle Sam.*
New York: Frances Foster Books, 2000.
Marcovitz, Hal. *Uncle Sam.* Philadelphia:
Mason Crest Publishers, 2003.
Yanuck, Debbie L. *Uncle Sam.* Mankato, Minn.:
Capstone Press, 2004.

On the Web

FactHound offers a safe, fun way to find
Web sites related to topics in this book. All of
the sites on FactHound have been researched
by our staff.

1. Visit *www.facthound.com*

2. Type in this special code:
1404847065

3. Click on the FETCH IT button.

Your trusty FactHound will fetch the best sites
for you!

Index

Look for all of the books in the American Symbols series:

Angel Island	The Liberty Bell	The Statue of Liberty
The Bald Eagle	The Lincoln Memorial	Uncle Sam
The Bill of Rights	Our American Flag	The U.S. Constitution
Ellis Island	Our National Anthem	The U.S. Supreme Court
The Great Seal of the United States	Our U.S. Capitol	The White House
	The Pledge of Allegiance